I Am Waiting

By Anne Meeker Watson
Illustrated by Nick Berman
Photographs by Jill Anderson

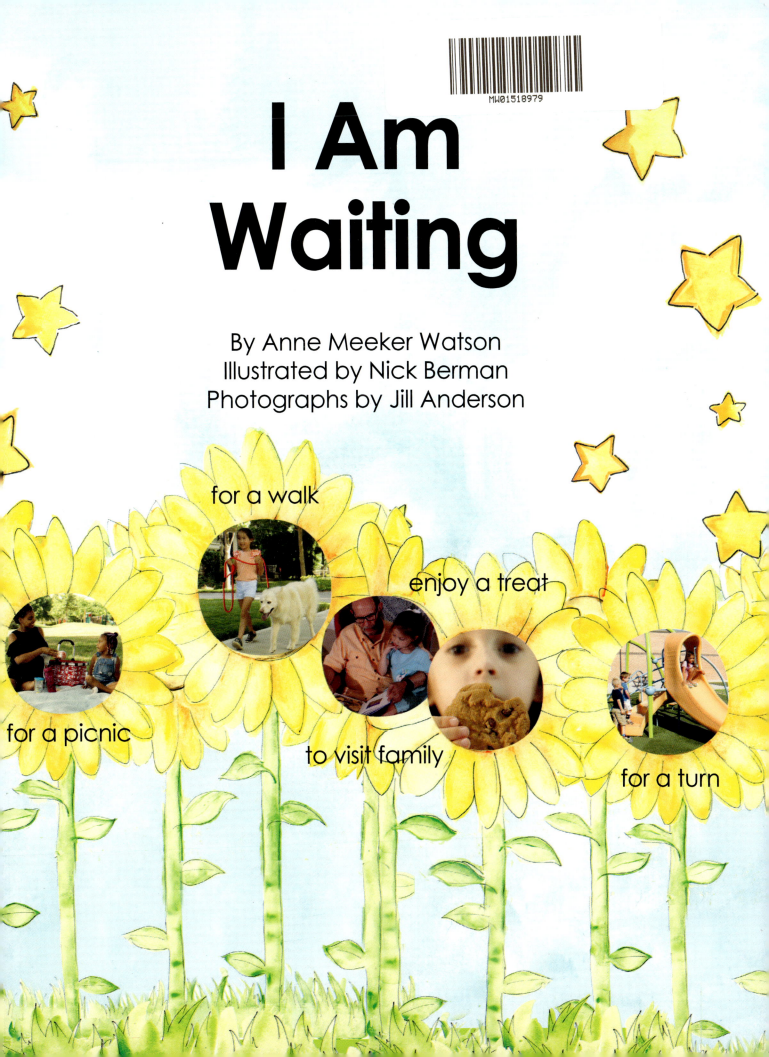

for a walk

enjoy a treat

for a picnic

to visit family

for a turn

I am waiting.

I am waiting.

I am waiting.

Now I clap
my hands.

I am waiting.

I am waiting.

I am waiting.

Now I stomp my feet.
Now I clap my hands.

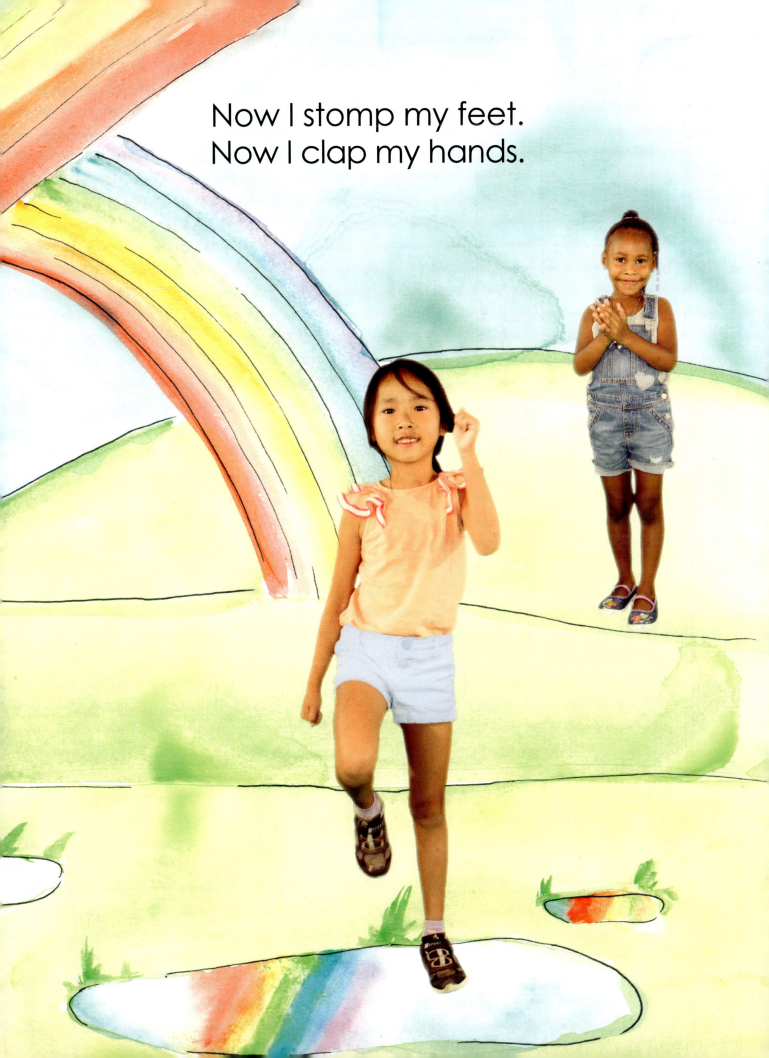

I am waiting.

I am waiting.

I am waiting.

Now I catch the stars.
Now I stomp my feet.
Now I clap my hands.

I am waiting.

I am waiting.

I am waiting.

Now I fancy
pants dance.
Now I catch the stars.
Now I stomp my feet.
Now I clap my hands.

I am waiting.

I am waiting.

I am waiting.

Now I dance
with you!

Patience
Activities to help young children learn and grow

He that can have patience can have what he will.
—Benjamin Franklin

Having patience and being able to wait are critical life skills. Guiding children in acquiring the inner emotional strength required to wait will help them think through situations, resolve problems, and cultivate the ability to self-soothe. Such skills are needed daily to have self-control, to take turns, and to delay gratification. They are also important skills for making and keeping friends.

The following fun activities will help you to teach patience and waiting to your children. By using these activities and by modeling patience in your own daily life, children will glean the essential skills needed for waiting and persevering.

MOVE YOUR BODY

On Your Mark, Get Set, GO! One of the simplest games to teach patience is this three-command start used in racing. The directions literally mean to: 1) stand in your lane or on your spot; 2) assume your starting position; then 3) take off! Ask your child to play this "game" in anticipation of running from one location to another. Model how to first stop, then assume a running posture with one foot in front of the other, and then run when you say the word GO. You can exaggerate the duration of each step by delaying the next verbal direction. Generalize these directions to other activities, like going up the stairs to bed or cleaning up toys. "You find the fun, and SNAP, the job's a game!" (Thank you, Mary Poppins.)

Red Light, Green Light. Choose one child to be the leader and have him stand with his back to the other players. All of the other players stand at a starting line with the goal of getting to the finish line where the leader is standing. The players walk toward the finish line when the leader says, "green light." When the leader says, "red light", the players must stop when the leader says, "red light." If the leader catches someone moving, he must send that person back to the starting line. The first person to cross the finish line wins and becomes the new leader. It takes patience to wait until the leader says: "green light!"

What Time is It, Mr. Fox? All of the players line up at one end of the room. The leader is "Mr. (or Miss) Fox" and stands near the finish line with his or her back to the group. The players yell, "What time is it, Mr. Fox?" and the leader responds with a time such as ten o'clock. The class then takes that many steps. After everyone takes their steps, they repeat the question and the leader responds with another time. However, each time they ask the question, the leader waits a few seconds longer before replying. When the players get close to "Mr. Fox," he or she responds by saying "midnight." The players then try to run to the finish line. Any players that "Mr. Fox" can tag are OUT!

LET'S PLAY AND PRETEND

Puzzle Present. Pick a puzzle, wrap each puzzle piece in wrapping paper, and place all of the pieces in a basket. Make sure that there is at least one puzzle piece per child. Have the children sit in a circle and pass the basket around the circle while music plays. The children should pass the basket until the music stops. When the music stops, the person holding the basket will pick a person in the group to select a present. The selected child will unwrap the puzzle piece and place it in the center of the circle. Repeat, allowing each new child who unwraps a puzzle piece time to put together the available pieces before continuing the game.

Doctor's Office. Whether in real life or dramatic play, one must wait when at the doctor's office. Set up a dramatic play area with a doctor's kit, an "examination" chair, and three or four chairs lined up to create a waiting room. Select one child to be the doctor first. Patients can read books while they sit in the waiting room. The doctor is required to fill out a form and take a phone call before seeing each patient. One by one the patients will get an examination by the doctor but will have to wait for the patient before them, the paperwork, and a phone call. After a child gets to see the doctor, they can become the doctor.

LOVING OTHERS…AND MYSELF!

Plant a Seed. Watching nature creates a fantastic opportunity to learn and wait at the same time. Have your child plant seeds and watch for growth. Together with your child, place three or four cotton balls in a quart-sized clear bag. Next, add several grass seeds, a flower seed or two, and two tablespoons of water. Lastly, tape the open bag to a sunny window. Now, wait and watch the seeds change in the days to follow.

Baking Cookies. Cooking can help children learn how to have patience to work through a multi-step process that ends with a great reward. Getting out ingredients, measuring and mixing, and patiently waiting through the baking process can be quite a tall order for a little person. Children must also follow directions, measure, and use their hands to complete the steps. However, the resulting cookies will be worth it!

Wait on Purpose. One of life's most important lessons is learning to delay our gratification. Help your child master this skill by intentionally requiring him or her to wait for something they want. By waiting, children learn that they can patiently wait to receive something they really care about. Their patience may require a short wait for a trip to the library on Saturday, or a long wait for birthdays, holidays, or adding a summer puppy to your family! Teaching this skill is one of the most loving and important things we can offer our children.

GET READY TO READ

Wait for It. This is a fun book time activity that will create excitement while waiting. Read a picture book aloud and when you get to the exciting part, close the book and announce, "we'll have to wait for it." This is a fun way to combine the love of reading and the reward of waiting. Some possible titles include:

☐ **Night Noises** by Mem Fox. Stop reading right before Lily opens the door to investigate the commotion outside.

☐ **Bear's New Friend** by Karma Wilson. Stop reading after the lines, "Come on outside. Then . . ." and allow your child to finish the sentence.

☐ **The Little Old Lady Who Was Not Afraid of Anything** by Linda Williams. Stop reading after the line, "What do you think she saw?"

MORE BOOKS TO READ

Check out these books about patience and waiting:

Are We There Yet? by Dan Santat
Bunny Cakes by Rosemary Wells
Harriet, You'll Drive Me Wild by Marla Frazee
Llama, Llama Red Pajama by Anna Dewdney
Waiting by Kevin Henkes
Waiting Is Not Easy by Mo Willems

ABOUT THIS ACTIVITY GUIDE

The goal of the activity guide is to share activities that you can enjoy with the children you love while connecting with them in a more meaningful way. Music combined with play, rich picture book literature and YOU as a child's play partner create the engagement a young child needs to learn and grow. My SING.PLAY.LOVE.® songs, books, movies and activities can be powerful tools for supporting the development—and delight—of your youngster.

Jennifer Ferguson does not mind waiting. She likes to wait for good movies to come to the theatre, cookies to bake, and exciting books to be released. She thinks the best "waits" in her life were waiting to meet her husband and waiting for her daughters to be born. As a child, Jennifer spent hours playing school with her trusty dachshund by her side. Now, she is a homeschooling mom, an enrichment teacher and a special educator who never tires of teaching. With another dachshund sidekick by her side, she loves creating fun lesson plans using books, music and games for her students of all ages and abilities.

I Am Waiting

Anne is not very good at waiting. She wants what she wants when she wants it. She often reads this book to herself, as a reminder that patience is a virtue.

Anne Meeker Watson, Ph.D., MT-BC is a singer/songwriter, music therapist and teacher of little children, as well as grown-ups who work in early childhood education. Her job is to make cool stuff to share with kids and their caring adults.

Jill Anderson thinks waiting is hard, but she keeps trying! Her loves, the art of photography and the science of early childhood education, both require copious amounts of patience and waiting. Says Jill: "If it is worth having, it is worth waiting for!" When not working on her patience, Jill can be found playing in her nature preschool classroom with young children or photographing beauty in the great outdoors.

Nick Berman has never been a very patient person. Luckily, he's had some very patient people in his life to help him along. Nick is a graduate of the University of Kansas with a degree in illustration. He has a love for working with children and telling stories, and he knows that even though it's hard, most of the best things in life require some patient waiting.

SING.PLAY.LOVE.® educational products – including songs, music videos, picture books and other resources – are fun and engaging for both children and their caring adults. When used in combination, **SING.PLAY.LOVE.**® products provide the repetition and enrichment young children need to practice new skills and prepare for kindergarten success.

Visit **SingPlayLove.com** for more fun products to support early learning, kindergarten readiness and FUN.

Copyright © 2021 Anne Meeker Watson
Illustrated by Nick Berman
Photography by Jill Anderson
Production design provided by Deidre Hof

Library of Congress Control Number: 2017910647

ISBN: 978-1-945598-58-6

SING.PLAY.LOVE.® **BOOKS** published by Meeker Creative LLC, Kansas City, Missouri.

SingPlayLove.com